A Long Walk

Lewis Pipkin

BookLeaf Publishing

India | USA | UK

Presentation by *BookLeaf Publishing*

Web: www.bookleafpub.com

E-mail: info@bookleafpub.com

ISBN: 9789363312975

First edition 2024

For my Why.

ACKNOWLEDGEMENT

I would like to thank my family. My wife, Kristi, and my sons Colton and Emmett. You have celebrated and pained with me. I am greater and grateful because of you.

PREFACE

This collection of poetry hopes to conjur the emotions we feel, memories we make, and experiences we have along the way. Blazing the trail for our "walk".

Tears

White on White
quiet as shallow breath
clinging to each other as long-lost friends

A village of snowflakes gathering,
prepare for the concert of winter.
Songs of sparrows shatter silence and sing of
spring

They whisper their goodbyes.
Never again seen
Hug into tears and fall into lakes and streams
Pine trees weep for winter's passing.

Fight

No one talks
No whispers
No quiet conversations
Sirens and screams are sinews of service

A Brother is bleeding
Just don't quit
Just dont stop
Don't beacon the bagpipes bellow

Blood dries black on asphalt
Visit the fight with fight
Comfort yourself with pain
Fill your lungs with breath and blood

Promises were made
"I will always come home"
Remember your "why"
They carry more than your last name
Swallow your teeth and fight

The sun rises again without regard
Face it and find your piece of peace
It's there, clear and calm
Celebrate the night and hold the light

hold the light...

BITCH

4

A look alone might bring a broken bone
If she's a bitch, a stitch
a sigh=   an eye
a tear=   an ear
More soap?
NOPE!
"MEOW"   OW!!
This is my life now...
I run
        I hide

                screaming inside..

If I get it wet, it's a losing bet

When giving the cat a bath...

Eros

Beauty
The subtle arch of your calf compassing your
thigh
Mapping directions to your hip
Covered by silk and breath
Journeying eyes pass your ribs and secrets to
unfold
Lips on your collar land cushioned kisses on
your neck
Your pulse felt with every caress

Don't hide anything...
Don't shy...
Bluest eyes close with sighs on my skin
Aches of anticipation make hearts quicken...
Too fast to go slow
Too savory to go fast
Quiet
Quiet...
Silent as eyes seeing
Dreaming without sleep
Studying this wonder
Memorizing every freckle...
Connecting dots for memory
Show me you...

Slow...slower...slowly...
Whispers without words
Soft... softer...
Intertwined like anchient vine
Poised for sweetest wine
Wishing for another drop to touch my lips
Yearning
Kissing
Desiring
LOVE...

?

Forging a path
in worn out shoes.
Choices ahead
Which do I choose?

Where to go?
Who to see?
What to do?
What to be?

What to hope?
Who to love?
What's below?
Whats above?

Where to start?
Where to end?
Who's an enemy?
Who's a friend?

Where to build?
Who to touch?
What's enough?
What's too much?

What to take?
What to give?
How to die?
How to live?

What to feel?
What to think?
What to eat?
What to drink?

Like those to come
and those long gone
These choices are mine
and mine, alone.

Pigeon?

(I asked my young son to give me 5 words)

BUCK drives to the river.
Now buck drives a big, bad, blue TRUCK!
Buck drove this truck into some MUCK.
Buck's truck got STUCK in some river muck
Buck thunk on his muck-stuck truck.
"How can I get my muck-stuck truck unstuck
from the muck?"
He heard the crack of a "quack" break through
the settling silence.
Suddenly... it hit him and he knew!
A PIGEON!
a PIGEON will help BUCK get his
MUCK-STUCK TRUCK un st..u..ck.....
Wait.... no....   never mind...

Insomniac

Tired
Drifting from dream to dream
Monotony of clock clicks
like things of lives past...

Playing games with digital time now
2:43 A.M.
2:44? NOW!
no.....NOW!...
no... NOW!
YES! Time changed.
Have I?

Celebrating an exhausting victory.
Play again?

As a child, I slayed my dragons
Over time, dragons become demons and stare
back, from darkness, unafraid
studying the blue-green-grey in my eyes.
Another yawn brings more tears.
Colors become clearer in the mirror.

This stranger's face is old..
Wrinkled and tainted with forced decisions and
loss.
Living is not for the dead
Let them go...
Let them bury themselves
Stop digging and shatter my shovel
Walk away
Better yet, run...
to slumber.

A forever game of hide and seek
Darkness upon darkness of dreams seeking
Hope of hiding in the light
I am haunted
2:49 AM
Tired.

Waves

A wispy mist of rain
like static on the radio
draws attention to birds
circling in their over-Earth playground.

Not quite fog
Too heavy
It falls and feeds the sand and fragile grass

I shrug the blanket higher on my shoulders
to keep my neck dry.
Only noise is from
wave on wave on wave on wave on wave...
Stacking like ovation
Standing
Disappearing the same

Uncovering memories
Memories of tiny toes ran through and washed
clean
Riotous laughter and squeals of joy
chiseled into stone gray matter

I face the wind and the rain
Waves wash over toes
I am cleansed and I dance again.

A Long Walk

I was told I had it.
Spoken like a terminal diagnosis
So what!
I pen my own ending...
Trauma stacked up like a snow storm
Heavier and heavier...
There's a long walk ahead!
A long walk indeed...   a journey of steps...
One, then another, another still.
Bring me a blanket,
a shovel
a match and some wood
I'll light a spark!
It only takes a spark!
I will hybernate and wait for spring...

All things grow in spring
new grass... miles and miles of it...
that new, vibrant, living green!
Saplings
New birth
new leaves and ME...
Bent under the weight of winter
Not broken, not smothered...
Only a spark to erase the dark...

I'll wait 'til the thaw
and emerge anew.

Twilight

A dragonfly dips for a sip of life
while the mourning dove calls.
Playful sparrows privately flirt
amongst shrouded branches.

The softest of kisses
show love from the wind
moving leaves like a chorus line
and dance to the birds' song

The world is taking a breath
One eye open
Not quite day
Not quite night

A staring contest between them
Repeated rituals over millennia
Drops of dew
Poised to fall

Holding fast
Lingering
Not ready to pass
Waiting

Like diamonds at dawn reflecting the victor...
The day has emerged like others
Quiet fanfare beautifully orchestrated
The masterpiece of God's opus.

Sons

I have been the harbinger of my hope
the champion of my spirit
the conqueror of my soul
the victor of my life...

Alas, mine is mine no longer...

I am now a harbinger of you
a champion of your youth
a conqueror of your fears
a victor of your doubts...

Behold your greatness
You stand mightily among giants
You sail above the sun
Arms spread, wings wide
Unlike Icarus, you soar

You are a legend
Your legacy has begun
You...
You Leaders
You Titans!

You, masters of your destiny,
Grow strong
Slay the demons that darken your path
Embrace your journey and Soar!

Nutcracker

The
precisely
perfectly
placed
punch
of
a
pudgy
paw
pounded
by
a
pouty
and
pernicious
toddler
placed
Papa
in
a
prayer
position.

Music

Music begets thought
Thought begets memory
Memory begets emotion
Emotion begets change

Music births rhythm
Rhythm creates dance
Music gives awkward boys
a fighting chance.

A chance to woo that unattainable girl
To take her hand, and make her your world.
To ignite a dream where you are lighter than air
A dance everyone watches, where neither one
cares

Music foreboding
There's danger about
Creak the door open slowly...
Wait! Stop! Watch out!

Whimsical chirping of piano keys
Whisps you away to a land of fairies
Where pirate ships sail and swords are drawn
Where treasures await and you sail at dawn.

Music, solemn, somber and slow
Might mean it's time to let someone go.
Fold your black umbrella and cry in the rain
Let it wash over your heart and guide you
through pain

Organ pipes play
for God, seated on high.
Choir voices sing His praise
with hands raised to the sky

Music enhances that which we feel
It's life seen clearer, more sincere, more real
Tap a foot, hum a tune, give a shimmy or shake
for music is the marrow of this journey we take.

Be Kind

22

The smallest acts
switch on the brightest lights
in the darkest corners

Therafish

The wetter, the better
Rescued from the clutches of some tween
Jack-Ass.
Poking holes and leaking life from your
bag-home

Fair fish unfair for fish
Life bartered for a well placed ping-pong ball
Colored rocks and plastic trees make home
Two years past

You feed on flakes with fluttered fins
You seem happy but don't show it
Your memory is limited but your id is cared for
We chat often and I have yet to win the staring
contest.

Bizarre

"Bizarre" was what you said
Perhaps speaking of a life lived
Last words whispered of some Residents' song
You drove mom to the hospital when she was
bursting with me
Stories of the flu and Spider-Man
You educated me on comics, comedy, music and
movies where everyone melted
You moved, married, mated and missed
birthdays.
Made up by moving me in more than once
A constant lighthouse
Both divorced, we moved on
like towering oaks in the same breeze
Love lost and life's loss
You smoked weed and I drank
we met in the middle for Simpsons, Sandman
and Scripture
This time, I moved, married, mated and missed
birthdays.
You loved my family as yours
like Christ loved the church
You never could tell a joke, though laughed like
you could
You learned to cook at 60

You punched me once.
Only once...
Violence was not your milieu
You sang off key and played using chords.
Bob and John decorated your office and filled
your soul.
Your words faded to theirs and your genius
inspired.
Our breaths now echo yours and your words
whisper in our memories
These breaths remind us of who you are.
I can't use the word "were" because these
whispers keep you alive.
We breathe the life you breathed into us.

Marshall Lee Pipkin 1959-2022

Paranoid

It's winter and I'm sweaty
Too sweaty to be ok...
I can hear my heart beating from across the
room.
Will it stop?
Or burst like a overfilled water balloon?
Heart attack?
Stroke?
Some new condition that medicine isn't aware
of?

I know...
I'll step outside into the fog to cool off.
It's so cold.

Why am I still sweaty?

I know...
I'll strip to my boxers and let the cold wash over
me
Nope, no luck, not fast enough
still sweaty...

I know...
I'm 6 feet from the pool edge

I'll just sneak over to the edge and dip my head.
Wait... If I dip my head, I'll fall in
If I fall in, I'll die.

I know...
I'll lay down and creep to the edge.
Just don't look down
I'll splash with my hands just a little bit
Just enough to wet my scalp

But,
What if I slip in?
Then what?
I'll drown...

My wife will find my bird-pecked corpse in a
week...
Also, if I fall in, I can't scream.
No one hears screams under water...
Have I forgotten how to swim?
The pool isnt that deep....
Nope! Won't try it. Can't. I'll DIE!

I'm still so sweaty...

6 feet away is too close
La Llorona is bound to drag me to a watery
grave.
Perhaps I should retreat to the safety of inside?

Tell my wife?
Risk a hospital for the insane.
Straightjackets, padded walls and drinking my
meals...

Wait...

Where is my heartbeat?

I'm clearly dead.
Do dead people sweat?
Sweat is my proof of life...
I am so fuckin' alive!

Breathe in
Breathe out
and live to sweat another day.

Lying Mirror

I am not wearing my skin today
It doesn't look like me
Not my eyes, the mirror lies
It cannot be me...
Not my hair, there's too much gray
Time has stolen my youth away
Whose hands are these?
Whose lips and tongue
The memories reflected
are of me, but young.
Age crept in
while I was asleep
The price of life
is much too steep
Graciously, gratefully
I accept my fate
To start living, not just existing
before it's too late...